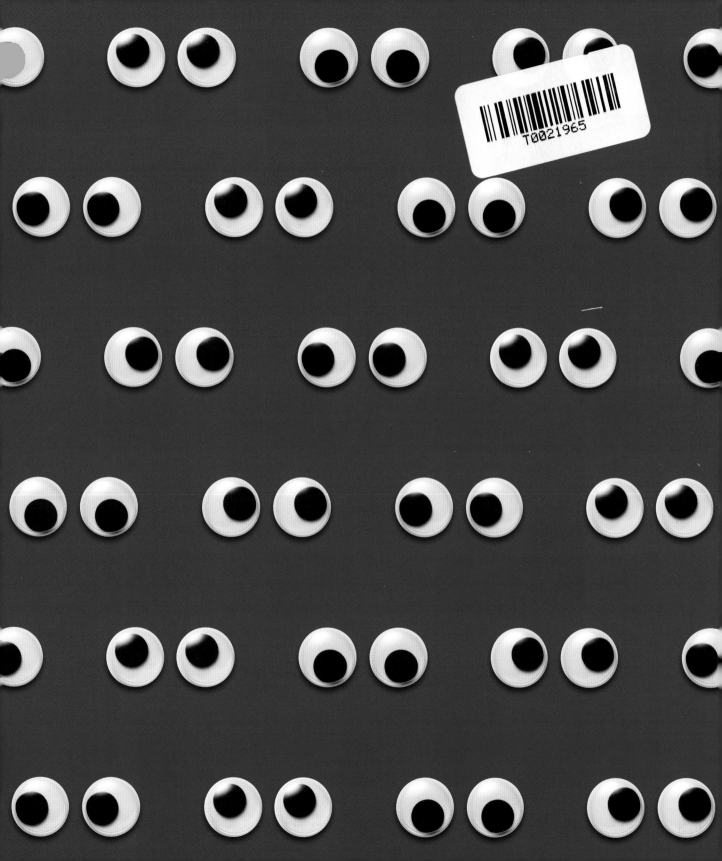

Copyright © 2024 by Kari Lavelle
Cover and internal design © 2024 by Sourcebooks
Cover images © Getty: Andrey Nekrasov, Diane Labombarbe, Edwin_Butter,
imageBROKER/Mara Brandl, MirageC, Ruslan Bardash, stephankerkhofs,
Takeshi Sasanuma/500px, Tambako the Jaguar, tane-mahuta; Robert Whyte.
Internal images © Alamy: Blue Planet Archive, Jason Ondreicka;
Daniel Kronauer; Getty: Andrey Nekrasov, Diane Labombarbe,
DNK-KolyaN, Edwin_Butter, GlobalP, imageBROKER/Mara Brandl,
MirageC, Romeo Ninov, Ruslan Bardash, stephankerkhofs, Takeshi
Sasanuma/500px, Tambako the Jaguar, tane-mahuta; Robert Whyte.
Illustrations by Michelle Mayhall/Sourcebooks

Published by Sourcebooks eXplore, an imprint of Sourcebooks Kids
P.O. Box 4410, Naperville, Illinois 60567-4410
(630) 961-3900
sourcebookskids.com

Cataloging-in-Publication Data is on file with the Library of Congress.

Source of Production: 1010 Printing Asia Limited, Kwun Tong, Hong Kong, China
Date of Production: September 2023
Run Number: 5035153

Printed and bound in China.
OGP 10 9 8 7 6 5 4 3 2 1

BUTT OR FACE?

REVENGE OF THE BUTTS

KARI LAVELLE

sourcebooks
eXplore

Can you tell
which end
you're
looking at?

From their heads to their tails, a creature's features are essential for their survival. Just like every part of your body serves a purpose, every part of an animal's body is important too, even their faces and butts! Animals have evolved to thrive and survive and scientists study how their features help them adapt in the wild.

When you look at these close-up photos, can you tell the difference between animal butts or faces?

Take a seat and get ready to play BUTT or FACE!

Let's start with this picture.

Do you think this is a

BUTT or a FACE?

Did you recognize the BUTT of the Indian peacock?

BUTT   TAIL FEATHERS

The famous biologist Charles Darwin suggested that male peacocks have those exquisite eyespots on their feathers to impress female peahens. Other scientists suggest that they might also use their feathers to evade predators. Either way, when this butt struts, the *eyes* have it on this beautiful behind!

Is it a

BUTT or FACE?

Those adorable faces use their strong, sharp teeth to help them eat fruit and crush hard shells.

It's the FACE of a white-faced saki monkey!

Despite their name, females have brown, gray, or red fur on their faces, not white. Only the males have white fur on their faces. Male or female, this monkey's face is *furry* cute!

White-faced sakis are nicknamed "flying monkeys" because of their amazing jumping abilities. They move from tree to tree, sometimes leaping up to thirty-three feet! That's as tall as the highest diving board at the Olympics!

Is it a
BUTT

or
FACE?

It's the FACE of the spicebush swallowtail caterpillar!

Scientists think these big, black-and-yellow eyespots on a caterpillar might trick predatory birds into thinking it's a slithery snake. Fake eyes that look like a snake? *Hissss*-terical!

Do you think it's

a BUTT or FACE?

It's the BUTT of a giraffe!

Giraffes often use their posterior
as a pillow when they sleep. They only need
about four hours of sleep a day. That patootie
provides a perfect place for a power nap!

Is it a
BUTT

or
FACE?

It's the FACE of the dugong!

Like its cousin the manatee, the dugong is a gentle giant of the seas. Fully-grown dugongs can weigh around eight hundred pounds, some as heavy as two thousand pounds! Unfortunately, the dugong is vulnerable to extinction. Dugongs eat seagrass and seagrass is affected by changes in the ocean. If humans don't fight against climate change, this species will be du-*gone*.

Is someone spying on us?

Do you think this is a

BUTT or a FACE?

This is the BUTT of the alien butt spider!

Scientists suggest the markings on the back of this spider's bottom make it look bigger to scare off predators. One thing is certain, this spider's booty is *out of this world!*

What do you notice in this photo?

Do you think it's a

BUTT or FACE?

Can you believe it's the BUTT of the *Nymphister kronaueri* beetle attached to an ant's BUTT?

Yep, double the derrieres! This beetle is so sneaky—it attaches itself to an ant and tricks the ant into transporting it around the ant colony. It even recreates the smell of an ant's patootie!

It's the FACE of the saiga antelope!

Its nose warms the air it breathes during cold winters and filters dust kicked up in their dry grassland habitat. Its wiggly nose actually moves like an elephant's trunk!

The saiga antelope doesn't suck up water through its large nose and squirt it into its mouth like an elephant does, though. It drinks water through its mouth.

To win over mates, males shake their noses to make a blubbery sound. The squishiest-sounding noses are selected by the females. It's *snot* easy to pick these noses—hopefully she *nose* what's attractive!

What do you see here?

Is it a

BUTT or a FACE?

It's the BUTT of the giant leaf-tailed gecko!

This reptile's body mimics the leaves and bark of a tree. Leaf-tailed geckos can also completely flatten their bodies against a tree, making it even harder for predators to find them. If a predator discovers them, they have another trick up their sleeve: they open their jaws to reveal a bright red mouth, sometimes even releasing a scream! These geckos just want predators to *leaf* them alone and *bark* up another tree!

Instead of using their tail to swim like most other fish do, the warty frogfish uses its gills to propel itself in the water.

It's the FACE of the warty frogfish!

Aren't you lured in by this beautiful face? The warty frogfish hopes to trick their prey by using its escae, a lure that looks like a worm, squid, shrimp or other small fish. Its mouth opens up extra wide so that it's able to eat fish that are the same size!

FACE THE FACTS

Frogfishes have the cool ability to change colors over time to camouflage themselves, mostly dependent upon the coral colors around them. This creature's ability to match its surroundings is impressive—warts and all!

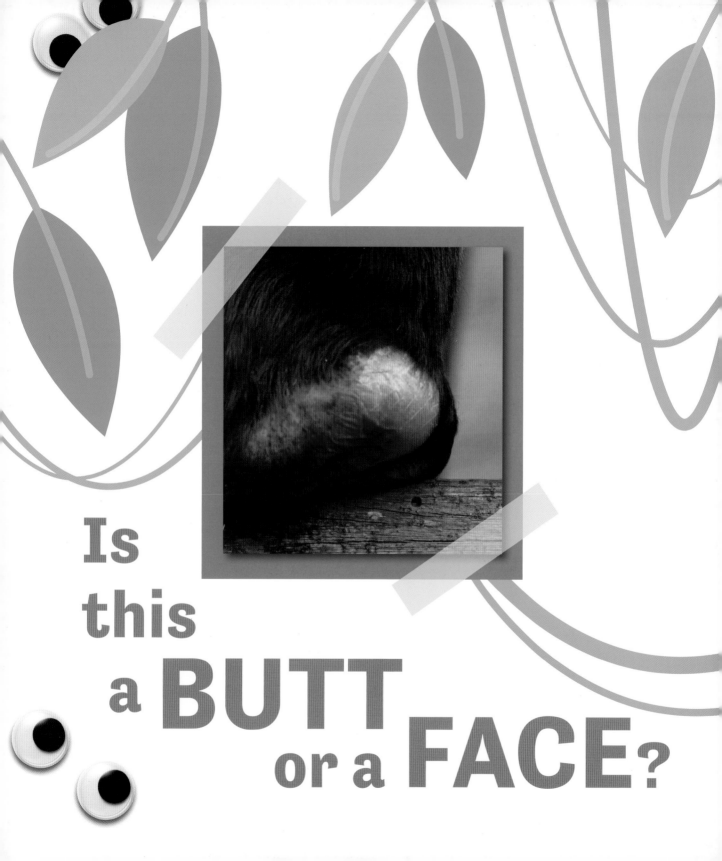

Is this a **BUTT** or a **FACE?**

BEYOND
THE
BACKSIDE

These monkeys are very affectionate with each other and love to snuggle. Butt-sniffs and friendly embraces are typical in their communities. They even ask for hugs by smacking their lips!

Yep! It's definitely the BUTT of a Celebes crested macaque!

And what a hiney! Scientists think those bodacious buns help attract mates.

BEYOND
THE
BACKSIDE

These mammals eat over one hundred different types of fruit. When they poop, they help scatter seeds that might become their future food source someday!

Is this a BUTT

or a FACE?

It's the FACE of an axolotl!

Axolotls have the coolest ability to regenerate their body parts, including their brain! Scientists hope that by learning about the axolotl, it will help improve medical technology for humans. These scientists will *axolotl* questions to learn about this animal's remarkable trait to heal itself!

FACE THE FACTS

Those feathery protrusions around their head are their external gills. They allow axolotls to breathe underwater.

FACE THE FACTS

This critically endangered amphibian is exclusively aquatic and only found in a single lake south of Mexico City!

Do you feel like an expert now?
Try this last one.

Is this a BUTT

or a
FACE?

Trick question! Neither!

This is a moon jellyfish, but because it's not a fish, some people call it a moon jelly. This moon jellyfish doesn't have a butt or a face (or a brain, or a heart)! Even though moon jellyfish don't have a face, they have eight rhopalia, sensory organs they use to see, smell, taste, and feel what's around them. Its mouth receives food and is actually the same body part that poops out the waste!

Doesn't nature have the silliest sense of humor?

Each of these butts and faces has unique features that help an animal survive. The next time you see a critter in nature, get curious about their characteristics and think about how their appearance helps them.

You never know, their face might save their butt and their butt might save their face! Either way, these butts get the last laugh!

AUTHOR'S NOTE

The idea for this book originated from an article I read about farmers in Botswana. Farmers paint eyes on the behinds of cattle to scare away predators, like lions. Painting the cattle helps the farmers keep their livestock safe. It also helps the lionesses—angry farmers were hunting the endangered species to protect their livestock. As I read the article, I thought about how the lionesses had to ask themselves "Is that a butt or a face?" when they approached the cattle, leading to the concept of this picture book.

FOURTH-GRADE KARI

GROWN-UP KARI

Photo © Mary Beth Huerta

ABOUT THE AUTHOR

This is the FACE of Kari Lavelle as a fourth grader. Kari had so much fun sitting on her BUTT, learning wacky facts about animals and writing this book. She's also the author of *We Move the World*. Kari lives in Austin, Texas, with her husband, their two kids, and their dog, Dobby (who has a very cute BUTT and FACE).